ASPIRATIONS

A personal collection of poems, proverbs and quotations

Written and compiled by Derek Dobson

Published by
Runnymede Publishing
173 Widmore Road
Bromley
Kent BR1 3AX

020 8
Phone: ~~0181~~ 460 1215
Fax: 0181 460 0999

ISBN: 0 9524486 1 0

'Aspirations' follows my first book entitled 'Inspirations' and is similar in its theme of recognising the sadness and problems in life but with a strong and positive optimism for the future. Some of the contents include passages received from readers of 'Inspirations' who felt that they would like to share words that have given them comfort at emotional times in their lives.

"All a poet can do today is warn. That is why the true poets must be truthful", wrote Wilfred Owen one of the most notable poets of the First World War. Truth is sometimes difficult to tell in a poem especially when it revives painful memories.

Likewise, an honesty and acceptance of the difficulties that we each face is not easy but, with hope as our guide, sensitive words can often provide the strength needed to meet and overcome such adversities.

Problems and the emotions which they create are all meant for a reason. As we leave behind each obstacle placed in our path, we can look back and realise how much stronger and wiser we have become; how much more compassionate and understanding we are and how much richer life is. No tear is wasted.

I hope that the following passages will help provide courage, comfort and consolation to those in need - especially to anyone who is, or feels, alone and has no one to talk to or confide in. The world can be a lonely place at times.

They are not necessarily my words; for words belong to us all and should be enjoyed by all.

DEREK DOBSON

"It is a good thing for
an uneducated man to read
books of quotations."

SIR WINSTON CHURCHILL
'My Early Life'

A fool will lose tomorrow
reaching back for yesterday

• LEARNING •

After a while you learn the subtle difference between
    holding a hand and chaining a soul.
You learn that love doesn't mean leaning
    and company doesn't mean security.
You begin to learn that kisses aren't contracts
    and presents aren't promises.
You begin to accept your defeats
    with your head up and your eyes open;
    with the grace of an adult, not the
    grief of a child.
You learn to build all your roads on today
    because tomorrow's ground is too uncertain
    for your plans.
After a while you learn that even sunshine
    burns if you get too much.
So plant your own garden and decorate
    your own soul instead of waiting for
    someone to bring you flowers.
You will learn that you really can endure;
    that you really are special and
    that you really do have worth.
So live to learn and know yourself and
    in doing so, you will learn to live.

ANON

To love another person
is to see the face of God

Truth is always the right answer,
for it cannot be disputed

DD

The Life that I have is all that I have
and the Life that I have is yours,
The Love that I have of the Life that I have
is Yours   and Yours   and Yours.

The Sleep I shall have
The Rest I shall have
Yet death will be but a pause
For the peace of my years in the long green grass
will be Yours   and Yours   and Yours.

ODETTE HALLOWES WARTIME CODE
(Died 16.3.95 - Aged 82)

Team-work is essential - it allows you to blame others!

DAVID BROWN

• THE BEATITUDES •

Now when he saw the crowds, He went up on a
mountainside and sat down. His disciples came
to Him, and He began to teach them, saying:

> *"Blessed are the poor in spirit,*
> *for theirs is the Kingdom of Heaven.*
>
> *Blessed are those who mourn,*
> *for they will be comforted.*
>
> *Blessed are the meek,*
> *for they will inherit the earth.*
>
> *Blessed are those who hunger and thirst*
>   *for righteousness,*
> *for they will be filled.*
>
> *Blessed are the merciful,*
> *for they will be shown mercy.*
>
> *Blessed are the pure in heart,*
> *for they will see God.*
>
> *Blessed are the peacemakers,*
> *for they will be called sons of God.*
>
> *Blessed are those who are persecuted*
>   *because of righteousness,*
> *for theirs is the Kingdom of Heaven."*

MATTHEW 5 v 1-10

• LONELINESS •

What is this thing called loneliness?
That hitherto was not my business
It happened to others, but not to me
Yet now surrounds me, to create perpetual agony

Since my loved one left my side
What is there but tears to hide
Is there any point in going on?
Since he bad farewell and then was gone

Is it right I should bear such guilt?
When we had love that both us built
Why oh why did he go away?
There's nothing I wouldn't give for him to stay

They say I must forget and carry on
As though it were a simple song
What do they know of how I feel?
Of pain that time will never heal

When will this fiendish hell depart?
It takes away all meaning from my heart
Must I carry on alone?
Or is there someone to find my love a home?

At times my anger grows so strong
But thankfully it does not last for long
The thing I need the most is peace
In order to provide a merciful release

There is but one that I can turn to
Who hears my prayer as well as you
He takes away my loneliness
As did you with your happiness

DD

• WEEP NOT •

Weep not for mankind and his works of destruction
Of all nature's beings and their production.
Weep not for his failings, his lust and his greed
That seem everlasting and increase with his seed.

Weep if you must for all nature's wide kingdom,
For the trees and the flowers that fall 'neath man's blade
And for the birds and the beasts that called it their home,
And for all these beauties which do gradually fade.

Written by a father who was not
'without sin' - no different from
the rest of us.   R in P

If I have not humility,
    then how can I have understanding?

If I have not the ability to forgive,
    then how can there be reconciliation?

If I have not compassion,
    then how can I have charity?

If I have not love,
    then what have I?

DD

If you have a friend worth loving,
Love him, yes and let him know that you love him,
Ere life's evening, tinge his brow with sunset glow,
Why should good words ne'er be said,
Of a friend 'til he is dead?

THOMAS HUGHES (1822-1896)

Worry gives little things big shadows

ANON

• LOVE YOUR ENEMIES •

"You have heard that it was said, 'Love your neighbour and hate your enemy'. But I tell you: Love your enemies and pray for those who persecute you, that you may be sons of your Father in heaven. He causes his sun to rise on the evil and the good, and sends rain on the righteous and the unrighteous. If you love those who love you, what reward will you get? Are not even the tax collectors doing that? And if you greet only your brothers, what are you doing more than others? Do not even pagans do that? Be perfect, therefore, as your heavenly Father is perfect."

MATTHEW 5 v 43-48

A successful partnership consists of
compromise and communication

DD

• AUTOBIOGRAPHY IN FIVE SHORT CHAPTERS •

I go down the street.
There is a deep hole in the pavement.
I fall in.
I am lost ... I am hopeless.
It isn't my fault.
It takes forever to find a way out.

I go down the same street.
There is a deep hole in the pavement.
I pretend I don't see it.
I fall in again.
I can't believe I am in the same place.
But it isn't my fault.
It still takes a long time to get out.

I go down the same street.
There is a deep hole in the pavement.
I see it there.
I still fall in ... it's a habit.
My eyes are open.
I know where I am.
It is my fault.
I get out immediately.

I walk down the same street.
There is a deep hole in the pavement.
I walk round it.

I walk down another street..........

Wisely and slow, they stumble that run fast

WILLIAM SHAKESPEARE

There is a wisdom of the head
and a wisdom of the heart.
To which should we attach the most importance?
The head dictates what we should do;
The heart that we want to do.
Is it wiser to do what is right
Or is it better to create happiness?
Think carefully, for tomorrow we shall awake
and face the consequences of our decision.

DD

• AN ENGLISH ROSE THE WHOLE WORLD LOST. •

A candle in the wind, from which
    a flame burned so brightly,
Yet it was not to be,
    and extinguished o'so early.

A lily pure and white
    that was able to create so much light,
An acorn that became an oak
    but soft and warm when e'r she spoke.

Love and happiness will take her place
    yet nothing can replace her smiling face,
Not a day will pass
    when her memory shall not last.

An English rose the whole world lost
    that was plucked at such a cost,
How can it be that she should die
    whilst we continue to ask why, o' why?

A tribute to Diana, Princess of Wales

DD

*"Therefore do not worry about tomorrow,
for tomorrow will worry about itself.
Each day has enough trouble of its own."*

MATTHEW 6 v 34

A smile can hide
a thousand tears

DD

Do not stand at my grave and weep
For I am not there, I do not sleep.
I am a thousand winds that blow,
I am the diamond glint on snow.
I am the sunlight in ripened grain,
I am the gentle falling rain.
When you awaken in the morning hush,
I am the swift uplifting rush
of quiet birds in circled flight.
I am the soft stars that shine in the night.
Do not stand at my grave and cry
For I am not there, I did not die.

Do not stand at my grave and mourn
I am not there, my soul is borne
upon the whispering breeze that sighs
and tells its message to the skies.
I am the ripples upon the lake;
I am the colours the rainbows make;
I am the echoes booming round the hills;
I am the freshness of air that fills
each heart with joy. I roam abroad
in peace with all, in one accord.
Do not weep at my grave, my spirit has soared;
I am still alive, hand in hand with the Lord.

ANON

The second verse is rarely quoted

I disapprove of what you say,
but I will defend to the death
your right to say it.

VOLTAIRE (1694-1778)

• THE KNIGHT'S PRAYER •

God be in my head,
> *And in my understanding;*

God be in my eyes,
> *And in my looking;*

God be in my mouth,
> *And in my speaking;*

God be in my heart,
> *And in my thinking;*

God be at mine end,
> *And at my departing.*

This prayer is thought to be by
St Ormund, Bishop of Salisbury,
Chancellor to William the Conqueror.

When you don't pay the price,
you don't feel the cost

DD

LOVE IS....

Love is the most powerful emotion that will ever enter our body, mind and soul. It's loss can devour our very will to live and it's gain to create motivation for living to eternity.

It has been written about more times than there are grains of sand and thought of more than there are stars in the sky. Yet we take love so much for granted until, like our life, we are in danger of losing it.

The very thought of not being able to love someone close to us creates panic, insecurity and fear. For what is life if it cannot be shared and love if it can neither be given nor received?

Love has many forms as it reveals our innermost feelings for others, be they our mother, father, son, daughter, friend or foe.

"Love your enemies" did our Lord once say - how on earth can you love an enemy? This must surely be the hardest love of all; to love another whom we hate.

Perhaps a true story may best illustrate such love......

...It was a bitter and freezing Christmas Eve in 1914 somewhere in Flanders. The snow was being driven by a cold icy wind as men huddled together in trenches to keep warm. So far from home and loved ones; no fires allowed for fear of revealing their positions - their generals safe and warm in chateaus many miles away. Forgotten by the politicians at home who cared only for their own future a victory could bring.

Next morning the large red disc of the sun greeted them as it rose in the east. The wind and snow had gone and was replaced by brilliant sunlight. Not a sound could be heard - not even the birds which had long since fled the bullets and smoke of the battlefield. A desolate and uncompromising landscape now revealed itself. Was this really Christmas Day? A far cry from a stable in Bethlehem; with the enemy just yards away waiting to kill or be killed. This must be some kind of cruel joke; a dream perhaps, void of reality.

A lone voice then began to sing..."Silent night, holy night..." Quickly, others joined in and before long it built into a crescendo. Amazingly, the voices did not just come from the British trenches but also the German lines. As they sang in unison a strong feeling of togetherness was apparent. Gone were the feelings of anger and hate for each other, to be replaced by a warmth and empathy.

A football was then kicked into the air in a moment of forgetfulness. Two men jumped out of their trench without a thought of danger, only to be met by two German soldiers. A football match then developed as others joined in. Was this really happening? After a few minutes reality dawned and the opposing teams hugged each other with feelings never felt before and returned to their respective trenches.

A moment of mad, unashamed bliss, preserved in the annals of history but truly a case of ....'love your enemies'.

DD

Love can be so fair to some
and so cruel to others

We take sport too seriously
and life too lightly

JOHN ARLOTT

• ASK, SEEK, KNOCK •

*"Ask and it will be given to you; seek
and you will find; knock and the door
will be opened to you.*

*For everyone who asks receives; he who
seeks finds; and to him who knocks,
the door will be opened.*

*Which of you, if his son asks for
bread, will give him a stone? Or if
he asks for a fish, will give him a
snake?*

*If you, then, though you are evil,
know how to give good gifts to your
children, how much more will your
Father in heaven give good gifts to
those who ask him!*

*So in everything, do to others what
you would have them do to you......"*

MATTHEW 7 v 7-12

When you're in the driving seat,
it's very easy to become complacent.
It's not until the car stops that you
realise you need an engine.

DD

I asked for strength that I might achieve;
    I was made weak that I might obey.
I asked for health that I might do greater things;
    I was given infirmity that I might do better things.
I asked for riches that I might be happy;
    I was given poverty that I might be wise.
I asked for power that I might have the praise of men;
    I was given weakness that I might feel the need of God.
I asked for all things that I might enjoy life;
    I was given life that I might enjoy all things.
I have received nothing I asked for, all that I hoped for.
    My prayer is answered.

Reputedly written by a young soldier who received massive and
permanently debilitating injuries in the American Civil War.
He lived as a cripple the rest of his days, wrestling and waiting
for God to show his face, his purpose in it all.

Faithful friends are a sturdy shelter:
Whoever finds one has found a treasure

ECCLESIASTICUS 6 v 14

Tact is the art of making a point,
without making an enemy

• THE GIFT OF LIFE •

The gift of life is free so use it wisely and waste it not; you will not get a second chance. Never forget that people are more important than possessions. Possessions can be replaced; people cannot. Treat them well and you will be rewarded. It is by giving that you will receive. Remember what unites us and not that which divides us, for it is togetherness that creates strength, fulfilment and a love for one another. Savour and enjoy what you have today for tomorrow you may mourn its passing. Regrets can be our past but hope our future. Strive with all your strength to attain happiness for it can be as elusive as a butterfly. Remember at times of difficulty that without pain there can be no understanding of life and all that it provides; for we must sometimes suffer pain in order to learn. However, we then become wiser and more compassionate to our fellow beings. Remember, too, that whilst you cannot change the world, the world will change you. So when your life takes an uncertain path, hold it by the hand and it will lead you into your future, whatever that may be; it is not for us to choose our destiny. If you are fortunate, love will enter your life. Never, never take it for granted for it will be the most wonderful and powerful emotion ever to enter your body. Treasure and nurture such a feeling as though it were a priceless gift, for that is what it is. When you lose someone you love, no one can take away the pain. But never apologise for shedding a tear as you would not a smiling face. Grief needs to be expressed if we are to live again. And never take your health for granted for you have but one life to live.

DD 9.10.96 Kefalonia   Written on a day when our Lord
                                          chose to look over my shoulder

*No-one is indispensable but
some people are irreplaceable*

DD

I am but no different to a coin
For were it not so what a dull
                    person I would be
A head to provide reason, understanding
                    and wisdom
And a tail which gives humour, feelings
                    and a desire for life.

DD

• JUDGING OTHERS •

*"Do not judge, or you too will be
judged. For in the same way as you
judge others, you will be judged, and
with the measure you use, it will be
measured to you.*

*Why do you look at the speck of
sawdust in your brother's eye and pay
no attention to the plank in your own
eye? How can you say to your
brother, 'Let me take the speck out
of your eye,' when all the time there
is a plank in your own eye? You
hypocrite, first take the plank out
of your own eye, and then you will
see clearly to remove the speck from
your brother's eye."*

MATTHEW 7 v 1-5

Life and Love's last gift
is remembrance

• MARRIAGE •

*Now you will feel no rain, for each of you will be
shelter to the other.*

*Now you will feel no cold, for each of you will be
warmth to the other.*

*Now there is no more loneliness, for each of you
will be companion to the other.*

*Now you are two bodies, but there is only one life
before you.*

*Go now to your dwelling place, to enter into the
days of your togetherness,*

And may your days be good and long upon the earth.

ESKIMO POEM

• A MOTHER'S LOVE •

Our mother's love knew no bounds
It saw us through life's ups and downs
Gave comfort when a tear was near
Protected us from all our fears
From babes in arms we nurtured were
No sacrifice too great for her
From childhood into teens we grew
With troubles that were far from few
And still her love would constant be
No thought of self was plain to see
Not always in the best of health
And never having claim to wealth
She soldiered on from day to day
Coping with what came her way
To all in need her arms held wide
Embracing and yet slow to chide
Such joy, such happiness and more
Such memories for us to store
In years to come will hold us tight
And bring us comfort through the night
Until that day we'll meet once more
Our turn to knock on heaven's door.

LESLEY DOYLE

When you have nothing left
but GOD,
you become aware
for the first time
that GOD..........is enough.

ANON

• THE FUTILITY OF WAR •

Let me wake from this dire hell
The foul smell of rotting flesh
Mutilated bodies by the thousand
Wretched, writhing, distorted faces
- The stench of death is everywhere.

As humanity falls into the abyss of hell
I shout aloud for it to stop
A futile gesture in a world of hate
Yet so much empathy and forgiving love
- How can I disentangle peace from pain?

No guarantee there'll be a 'morrow
Tears and hope are all I have
Memories dissolving in a sea of despair
Pools of blood can I but see
- What will the future hold for me?

God be with me today, I beg
Eternal nightmares will not set me free
All tossed in the cauldron of war
To create a recipe of death
- Serving to consume the horrors of today.

The choking gas, the pounding shells, the smoke,
the noise, what have I done to deserve all this?
Dear Lord hear my prayer and set me free
That I may live to follow Thee.

DD

• INSPIRATION •

When my life is finally measured in
Months, weeks, days, hours,
I want to live free of pain,
Free of indignity, free of loneliness.
Give me your hand;
Give me your understanding;
Give me your love;
Then let me go peacefully
and help my family to understand.

Author Unknown
Taken from a Belarus Hospice publication.

Faith in friendship is putting your
hand out in the dark and finding it held

ANON

• LEST I BE ALONE •

Reach out and touch me O Lord
- That I may be filled with the strength to
stand alone,

Place your hand on my shoulder
- That I may feel your presence ever near,

Cast your shadow over my life
- That I may have the courage to carry on,

Walk by my side at times of despair
- That I may hold the hand of faith,

Enter my heart when I am rejected
- That I may feel the warmth of your love,

Be with me when I feel alone
- That I may have your companionship,

- For I know you are always with me.

DD

*It is in the
garden
of patience
that
strength
grows best*

ANON

· WISDOM ·

Blessed is the man who finds wisdom,
the man who gains understanding,
for she is more profitable than silver
and yields better returns than gold.
She is more precious than rubies;
nothing you desire can compare with her.
Long life is in her right hand;
in her left hand are riches and honour.
Her ways are pleasant ways,
and all her paths are peace.
She is a tree of life to those who embrace her;
those who lay hold of her will be blessed.

PROVERBS 3 v 13-18

Take this body O My Lord
For it is You who must decide
Is my faith a two edged sword
Or do I need You at my side?

Take these eyes O My Lord
For it is You who must decide
Is my sight to be restored
Or will You become my constant guide?

Take these ears O My Lord
For it is You who must decide
Does my hearing find a chord
Or do I need You to preside?

Take this life O My Lord
For it is You who must decide
Are my shoulders sufficiently broad
Or will I run away and hide?

Take this soul O My Lord
For it is You who must decide
Will my faith be just a fraud
Or in my heart will You reside?

DD

"I am the resurrection and the life.
He who believes in me will live, even
though he dies; and whoever lives and
believes in me will never die."

JOHN 11 v 25-26

• GOD'S WAITING ROOM TO HEAVEN •

Do we come here as a reluctant guest
    or simply to obtain eternal rest?
We are welcomed by strangers
    that will banish all dangers.
They come from nowhere to enter our lives
    and then become our faithful guides.
Without such angels how could we find
    a brand new life that hitherto was blind.

We come with bewilderment,
    uncertainty and torment,
Yet are transformed by the atmosphere we find,
    its happiness and love; all of a kind.
A ray of sunshine bursts through the clouds
    to create eternal hope unbowed
And reveals a whole new world
    that is bathed in sunlight now unfurled.

Each day comes and goes
    and of our future no one knows,
But one thing's for sure
    that's as good as a cure,
For what was a mountain to climb
    has become like springtime,
A whole new beginning
    that means we are winning.

DD   Dedicated to Hospices everywhere

*"Jerusalem is our heritage
as much as it is yours.
It was from Jerusalem that
our Prophet ascended to
heaven, and it is in
Jerusalem that the angels
assemble."*

Letter from Saladin to
Richard the Lionheart

DD - Memories of an
      unforgettable journey

• THANK YOU •

As the light dawns each morn
As darkness falls, around the moon
As the stars shine in the sky
And clouds, silently pass by
We thank you Great Spirit
For each day we are given
We thank you
For always listening
We give thanks to each other for understanding
No matter what another's standing
We thank the Wise Ones gone before
For allowing us 'vision'
Through that eternal door
We thank those in spirit for drawing near
Helping us at times overcome our fears
We thank nature for bringing each season
When times are troubled and we can see no reason
We thank our pets that have stayed by our sides
When many times, from pain, we hide
But most of all, we thank each other
For being there, to truly discover
Knowledge within to aid humanity
Spiritual eyes so we may 'see'
For if help we can offer
To lost, lonely souls
There is nothing greater
Than Love as the reward
And if the Love has reached within
Opened eyes, that once were dim
What an achievement there would be
If everyone understood the meaning of...
.....SPIRITUALITY.

SANDRA WILLIAMS

Life is eternal and love is immortal...
and death is but an horizon and the
horizon is but the limit of our sight.

ABRAHAM LINCOLN

• PAUSE FOR THOUGHT •

Pause for a moment if you will and think of the important things in life. Forget trivialities for they will always exist - precious moments do not and true values are often forgotten in the hustle and bustle of everyday life.

What of your future? Do not be afraid to put your hand into the pool of destiny and grasp the unknown for it is the thought of what may be that can create hope. As you slowly withdraw and open your hand, your future will be revealed and the ripples that flow outward will affect all who come into contact with you. The personality which you project will be reflected back in the response from others. Fire from within can generate a warmth that will radiate and attract others; but ice can create coldness and deter communication. It is the eyes that mirror the soul and the heart that reflects our true self.

As you receive so must you give back. The scales of life need to be balanced if values are to be preserved. For by taking without giving will result in a selfish and lonely being.

Let us be wise enough to accept each other as we are for we are all individually moulded by our own journey through life. As the fruit tree sheds the beauty of its spring blossom after but a short period of time, it nevertheless remains the same tree. Indeed, good nourishing fruit follows to provide sustenance for the remainder of the year. So, too, do people and we must not expect them to be as we would wish all the time. Perfection is an illusion.

In a world that appears to grow increasingly hostile, materialistic and uncaring, it is important to retain faith in others and confidence in yourself, for without either you will have difficulty in looking to the future. Do not be afraid to unchain your mind and let it go free for prejudices must be freely faced without suppression if we are to discover what is right and what is wrong.

We all need to grow, to have a reason for living and going on. As plants need light to live, so too do we - a light that changes our life and creates an inner peace and happiness. However, it can only be found within ourselves.......like the wind, we know not from where it comes and neither do we know where it will take us. Peace is worth more than you or I - it is beyond price; for with it we are able to understand the true values of life as for one brief moment the hand of God touches our shoulder.

When you look back on your life, have no regrets or feelings of guilt for we make decisions as the person we are at the time and not as the wiser person we later become. Our past becomes a constant companion as it accompanies us into the future. A loyal friend advising us in times of uncertainty and indecision. What to do and what not to do; for history has the benefit of knowledge and hindsight. Lessons that have been learned in the past provide wisdom for the future. Remember at times of difficulty that your life has already been planned; your future and destiny cannot be changed. 'What will be, will be.' An acceptance of this can provide peace of mind when we encounter troubled waters.

At times in our lives it can be a very lonely world no matter how many friends we have; we stand alone within ourselves. We desperately seek the motivation and reasons to go on. For what purpose has life if it ceases to provide the happiness which we so much desire? At such times, when we crave comfort, understanding and friendship, we tend to forget that each one of us often feels the same. Yet we are not alone if we but hold out a hand. It is only by communicating with one another that we begin to understand we each have feelings and how similar they are - for do we not all experience the joy of happiness, the pain of grief and the elation of love?

We were all born, we will all die and we were all put on this same earth by our maker - no man or woman is any greater or any lesser than another. We are but one in the mists of time.

DD

If you do not expect,
you will not become disappointed

DD

FAITH is...

Knowing
　　before it is done
Believing
　　before it is proven
Loving
　　before you are loved
Giving
　　before you have received
Faith is...
　　Trusting in God
- You are in my prayers.

ANON

• TOMORROW •

Clouds fill the sky;
Your life darkens and the world disappears;
Everything becomes totally meaningless.
- But, as with time, the clouds will pass and
    reveal the sun which was there all the time.

As you look into the sunlight, your face
    shines again whilst your shadow appears behind you.
The future beckons as you hold out a
    nervous and shaking hand.
One step at a time
    - One day at a time
Slowly but surely your strength will grow
    and slowly but surely life will grow.

There was a time when every day seemed like yesterday
But there will come a time when today greets tomorrow;
When your mirror becomes a window;
It is then that you will see your future
    and not reflect on the past.

Have Faith, have Courage and have Hope
    for you will survive.

DD

*"Only those who adapt
to change survive."*

CHARLES DARWIN

GRATEFUL ACKNOWLEDGEMENTS

Susan Dwyer

For assisting with the
production of this book

Angie Thick

My ever patient and
understanding secretary

Wilhelm Rauch
Pictor International   For supplying the
Jan Tove Johansson   superb and
Trudi Unger   inspirational
Charles Gupton   photographs
Art Wolfe (Cover)

David Brown
Lesley Doyle   Contributors
Sandra Williams

Scripture quotations taken from the
HOLY BIBLE, NEW INTERNATIONAL VERSION
Used by permission of Hodder & Stoughton Limited

Dedicated to all those who have 'lost' a loved one
whether it be through death or separation.
- You are not alone.

Every effort has been made to find the copyright owner of
the material used. However, there are a few quotations that
have been impossible to trace, and I would be glad to hear
from the copyright owners of these quotations, so that
acknowledgement can be recognised in any future edition.